JUST AS A HOUSE ON A FIRM FOUNDATION

Winifred Smith Eure

Roselle, New Jersey

Copyright © 2023 by Winifred Smith Eure

All Rights Reserved.

No part of this book may be used or reproduced by any means, graphic, electronic, or mechanical, including photocopying, recording, taping, or by any information storage retrieval system without the written permission of the publisher except in the case of brief quotations embodied in critical articles and reviews.

This is a work in nonfiction. This book was taken from the author's personal experiences, her memoir captured important segments from her life. Some names and identifying details of people described in this book have been altered to protect their privacy.

For more information contact:
Independent Authors Publications
PO Box 7062,
Roselle, NJ 07203
www.independentauthorspublications.com

Cover Design – Webprint Lab
Edited – Catherine Felegi

Print ISBN: 978-1-950974-19-1
Digital ISBN: 978-1-950974-20-7
Library of Congress Control Number: 2023915726

Just as a House on a Firm Foundation is dedicated to my family, the Smith family, my club sisters of the Martin Luther King Jr. Civic Club, the Pastor, First Lady, members of my church, Heard AME Church in Roselle, New Jersey, and anyone, young and old, who desires a closer walk with God.

Contents

Introduction 1

Have You Heard? 2

Religion and Higher Education 7

House and Church Foundation 10

To Young Adult Parents 15

Choosing God 20

Community Service 24

Taking Care of Oneself 30

Juneteenth and Father's Day 34

Fantasy vs. Reality 38

Helping Our Youth 41

Book Summary 47

About the Author 49

Introduction

Before you open this book, know that I am a senior citizen who is a lifetime member of an AME church in New Jersey. I don't sing in the choir, don't usher, and am not a trustee nor Steward, even though I did some of these things and more when I was younger.

Now, I have a BA in Sociology, an MA in Special Education, and a K-12 Teaching Certificate. I have no formal or professional religious training, but I am a child of God and have a long relationship with Jesus Christ. If that is enough to arouse your curiosity, then go ahead, open, and read this book.

Have You Heard?

I am a lifetime member of Heard AME Church in Roselle, New Jersey where we often use the phrase, "Have you heard?" Have you heard that a house built on a firm foundation will stand the test of time? Have you heard that when a house is a Christian home, it has an even firmer foundation and it, too, will stand the test of time? I have heard statements similar to these more than once.

In the midst of adversity and storms, the abiding of Jesus sees us through and enables us to experience comfort in the Holy Spirit. We are able to handle our daily tasks, responsibilities, and relationships to endure by faith and enjoy rest and relaxation.

God has been forever present in my life. As a child, He kept me in joy, living happily with family and friends. When I became a young adult, He chastised me and convicted me for my sinful nature, yet He did not condemn me. I turned to Him completely in repentance, asking for His grace and mercy. I wasn't "in the street," but my soul was in a dark place. Surely, He delivered me.

I confess that much later, I had to lose so much to gain more. I lost all my immediate family members and ultimately my husband, who was a Godsend, to death. In my own amazement, I am still standing and standing up for Jesus. He alone is the head of my life. That is not to say that I don't have friends and family who are positive influences and whose wisdom I seek from time to time.

In my first non-poetry book *Testimony, The Ts Have It*, I shared my struggles of being diagnosed with gastrointestinal problems, which according to my holistic doctor, was the basis for my mental health crisis occurring later. Through it all, I've been able, by the grace of

God, to maintain my home, a few choice possessions, and a life full of the love of family and friends and still enjoy some fun and pleasure. These illnesses, at worst, have caused me to feel humiliation and emotional pain more than anything else. Yet, one day, I was listening to the news and I heard talk show host Kelly Ripa say, "One thing's for sure - embarrassment won't kill you." Her words lifted me.

One day, my gastrointestinal doctor shared with me a story from his youth. He once knew a young girl in his neighborhood who, after showering thoroughly every morning, would walk to the corner to take the bus. By the time she got to the bus stop, she would smell. People think their problems are paramount to others or say, "My trauma trumps your trauma." Does it really matter? What's important is that you "hit your knees" and surrender to God and ask Him to come into your heart and soul if you haven't already. Most Christians know that when this occurs, don't expect an instant miracle, but rather wait on the Lord to answer you. What you need is not "As soon as possible faith," but "As long as it takes faith." Mark Batterson talks about this in his book *Draw the Circle*, which my pastor, Pastor Points, recommended to members of our Bible Study.

You may feel alone, even though you are surrounded by supporters. You may feel estranged, separated from them by what seems like a mystery. Just put on your walking shoes - not the ones you wear to a party or celebration, but your most comfortable ones as you prepare to walk into unknown territory.

Finding someone to share my life with, getting a rewarding job, and becoming an author of several books were ways in which God answered my prayers. I thought I had arrived and reached my destination. Although I could be a blessing to others, I realized through death, retirement, and a drought in my writing, that these were merely seasons of my life. I thought being a good wife, a competent and conscientious teacher, and an influential writer were my only God-given gifts. Recently, however, God has allowed me through the Holy Spirit to speak and share my experiences, my faith, and belief in God the Father, Son, and Holy Spirit with others through Bible Study with other church members and through fellowship. This is not a destination - just another stage of my journey.

Change is inevitable, but the love God has for us never changes. You will never be perfect, but He can perfect His work in you if you allow Him to abide. Like the scripture reads, "Abide in me and I in you. As the branch cannot bear fruit of itself, except it abide in the vine; no more can ye, except ye abide in me." John 15:4 (KJV) What a firm foundation when we completely trust the Savior and anchor our faith in Him above all else!

Religion and Higher Education

Several of the youth at Heard AME aspire to obtain higher education. Some have already enrolled in college. An education is a blessing not to be taken for granted or wasted. Like the United Negro College Fund motto says, "The mind is a terrible thing to waste." The experience of college - living on campus, meeting new people and making new friends, joining extracurricular activities, being intellectually challenged by professors, finding one's strengths and recognizing one's weaknesses, at times succeeding and at times failing, preparing for a place and space in the world - is the opportunity of a lifetime. I pray that they cherish the experience.

How can they balance the secular and the

religious life as they leave a strong spiritual foundation and enter an unknown worldly environment? They should simply ask God to give them guidance and direction and talk to Him about their hopes and wishes for the future. They should ask Him to plan, mold, and shape their trajectory, and share with Him any fears and anxieties they may have. Students should keep their Bible with them, whether they live at home or on campus. They should try to read a Scripture daily and pray upon waking and going to bed at night. Yes, I know this can be easier said than done when worldly matters are tugging at hearts and minds. They should try to make good choices and develop good habits. Boring? With these, a firm foundation is knocking at their doors. Falling? If he/she can't dust themselves off and get back up, they should ask Jesus to pick them up. I wish someone had shared these gems with me. Parents assume their offspring know these things, but it makes a difference when you hear them from someone you respect and love.

Some young people choose not to attend college. Through contacts and experience, they excel in the workplace beyond their own imagination. They discover their talents and gifts and find the application of them rewarding. Some find joy in their relationships with significant others or life partners, have children, and delight in parenthood. They may or may not have a college education.

The fact is, we are all different and yet we all can make a difference if we put forth the effort. God wants to bless us and wants us to be a blessing to others. This, too, is included in a firm foundation that we should seek to know and experience for ourselves. We want the pieces of our puzzles to fit together and hold together, not be loose and lose their design and splendor.

"...God, who started a great work in you, will keep it and bring it to a flourishing finish on the very day Christ Jesus appears." - Philippians 1:6 (The Message Bible)

House and Church Foundation

During hurricane and tornado seasons, we hear through the news that many homes are destroyed, causing residents to lose everything while others remain unscathed and standing. I read that the quality of building materials used in homes have an effect on their fate. I learned that "most well-built concrete structures can withstand a category 5 hurricane... When used in conjunction with modern building codes, brick homes" can remain standing when others on the same block might be destroyed. Houses built on firm foundations were more likely to survive. I believe our omnipotent and omnipresent God is in control. His will is done in the final outcome.

JUST AS A HOUSE ON A FIRM FOUNDATION

The Bible teaches that "our bodies are the temple of the Holy Spirit… that we should honor God with our bodies." 1Corinthians,6:19 (NIV). I believe that the building blocks of my temple are love, faith, trust, obedience, and self-control. This firm foundation houses worship, praise, prayer, purpose, and service. When we have this foundation on the inside, our physical homes should also reflect our love of the Lord and our desire to serve Him. Remember, "As for me and my house, we will serve the Lord." Joshua 24:15 (KJV)

The foundation I received as a child was an upbringing in the church. All of my brothers were brought up in the church, too. My father worked hard to provide for us. He only went to church about four times a year - Christmas, Easter, Men's Day, and Father's Day. When he became ill in his old age, he began to attend more often. My mother taught me the importance of prayer. I would pray at night before going to bed, and loved reciting in church for special days like Christmas, Easter, and Children's Day. I loved singing in the youth choir, too. I must confess, though, that I loved public school and achieving in school more than anything. I loved sports and played hard after school and on weekends in my neighborhood.

Church was ongoing for me but the church wasn't in me like it should have been. I remember starting a fight with another high school student who really had done nothing to me. I just heard rumors about her and a boy I liked. When I look back, I realize how foolish and wrong I was. I have repented to God for all my sins and He has forgiven me. I hope and pray that anyone who I may have offended in my past by word or deed will forgive me, too, just as I have forgiven others.

Just a few months ago, I celebrated my 72nd birthday. Reflecting on my life, I have found peace and joy in the company of family and friends, as well as offering service through community organizations like The New Jersey State Federation of Colored Women's Clubs where I am the historian, or The National Council of Negro Women - Roselle Section where I serve as vice president. I sometimes wish that I remained active in the Sunday Service such as singing in the choir, ushering, or becoming a Steward or Trustee. However, I became seriously ill during service one day and it spiraled into a mental health crisis. I had prayed to God for clarity, guidance, and direction. He led me to ministries outside the walls of the church. When I became a special education teacher in Newark, one of our former assistant pastors, the Rev. Alexzina Brown, told me the work I was doing was missionary work. I felt better about myself then. Today, I wonder where would I be had it not been for that early firm foundation in the church, the learning of the basics - "Do unto others as you would have them do unto you" and "Yes, Jesus loves me." The organizations I belong to now serve nursing home residents, the homeless, food banks, teachers, students, families, and individuals in need. We are a blessing to others as we have been blessed.

To Young Adult Parents

To young adult parents, I say to you - your children are and will be influenced by others throughout their lives. I needed the influence of others, not just my parents, to succeed. I needed and still need the teachers who so graciously befriended me and served as a vital example in my life. You want or expect and maybe have a vision that your children will do better in life than you. My parents never gave up on me, no matter how bleak things seemed at times. My mother prayed for me. Pray that your children will experience joy, love, faith, purpose, and peace, that they will know Jesus in the pardoning of their sins and as their very best friend and savior. Pray that their needs will be met and that they will experience at least some of the desires of their hearts. Give them a firm foundation that they will entrust to their children.

We in the AME church believe that a child's upbringing in Sunday School is necessary and important to their growth as Christians and adults. In Sunday School, they get the basics of a firm religious foundation. They learn all about Jesus and what it means to follow Him. They get the instruction and guidance from Christian teachers who teach, share, talk with them, set an example for them, and teach them leadership skills and teamwork strategies. The children learn how to give back to their communities. Begin a generational blessing in your family or continue that which was given you. This does not mean that the lives of your children will be trouble-free. Into each life, some rain must fall. We all experience trial and tribulation. We need a foundation - the rock of Jesus on which to stand throughout our journey - a pathway to Heaven.

Sometimes, on Saturdays, I watch *House*

Hunters. Couples and some singles are searching for starter or permanent homes. Sometimes, one partner is seeking an older home with charm and character, while the other wants a ready-to-move-in, newer, modern home. These shoppers look at location (close or not too far from work), the "wow" factor when they open the front door, an open floor plan, a fireplace, hardwood floors, a large master bedroom, two or more bedrooms, roomy closets, a bathroom with a shower and bathtub, preferably double sinks, updated kitchen appliances, light-colored cabinets, granite kitchen tops, a nice backsplash, a gas stove, and a finished basement. Some want a large backyard for entertaining. Others don't want the responsibility of having to upkeep a large yard. Most want to stick to a home within their budget while a partner may be willing to spend beyond the budget. It's a blessing to have the means to afford your dream home, whether you are young adults or a retired couple.

People spend ample time, effort, and money when looking for an attractive and comfortable space to live. I could not help but wonder as I watched this show, are these house hunters, with all their particular preferences, also concerned with the spirituality of their home, of putting time and effort into making God the center and the foundation upon which their home stands? Some people are fortunate enough to be born into a family of plenty, while some are born into a family of poverty or limited means. Whether or not you achieve financial security, it truly matters that you put God first, if you haven't already. I am reminded of the lyrics, "Some folks would rather have houses or land. Some folks choose silver and gold. These things they treasure and forget about their soul, I've decided to make Jesus my choice." It's ok to have nice things, to have plenty, but "to whom much is given, much is required." Luke12:48 (KJV) When God blesses you, you should be a blessing to others. I am going to be a positive thinker and believe that by providing a new home, these house hunters are thinking of blessing each other and their families because God has blessed them. I hope that they are dreaming of establishing a home with a firm foundation of belief, trust, and faith in Him.

Choosing God

In May of 2023, during Tuesday morning Bible study, we were studying Luke chapter 10. I did my homework and read ahead for the next week. I recall reading Luke 10:38-42 (NIV). The setting was at the home of Mary and Martha. Martha had opened her home to Jesus. Her sister, Mary, sat at Jesus's feet, listening to His words. "Martha was distracted by all the preparations to be made. She said to Jesus, "Lord, don't you care that my sister has left me to do the work by myself? Tell her to help." The Lord replied, "Martha, you are worried and upset about many things… Mary has chosen what is better and it will not be taken away from her." In this scripture, the words "Mary has chosen" speaks volumes to me.

God has given us and still offers us so much

- His instruction and guidance, His grace and mercy, the Holy Spirit and the fruits of the Spirit, and the gift of eternal life, to name a few. He has made it so easy for us. All we have to do is choose to accept or reject Him. When we choose Him, He comes into our hearts and we are in His heart, just like Mary. He was pleased with her. I don't mean to suggest that He rejected Martha. Rather, He corrected her for her worry and anxiety, and told her Mary had made a better choice.

This also reminds me of another scripture - "Which one of us by worrying can add a single hour to his (or her) life?" Matthew 6:27 (NIV). Mothers often worry about their children and grandchildren. Their love and concern for them often causes anxiety and stress, which can cause high blood pressure and other health problems. Because I am not a mother in the biological sense, it is probably easy for me to say this, but sometimes, we have to leave our loved ones in God's hands, distance ourselves, pray, and give them up to our Heavenly Father. You probably will agree that this is true for every relationship wherein one partner worries about another or they both worry. We all need that peace that the Bible tells us about - "the peace which passeth all understanding." Philippians 4:7 (KJV) We need this not only for our mind, but our body, which is the temple of God. Let us ask God to enable us to make good choices and practice good habits daily. If we fail one day, then the next day is our clean slate to do better.

Thus far, I have addressed several types of firm foundations in our lives:

1. The structure of the houses we live in.
2. The pervasiveness of Christianity in the home/family relationships.
3. The Christian upbringing of ones' children.
4. Treating our bodies as the temple of God.
5. The rock, Jesus Christ, in whom we trust and obey.

These may seem like shoes too difficult to fit, but we must use our shoehorns of faith, hope, and perseverance and these will fit comfortably.

Community Service

I belong to a community organization called the National Council of Negro Women (NCNW). For those who do not know, it was found in 1935 by Mary McLeod Bethune and presided over for more than 50 years by "the iconic" educator and activist Dorothy Height. Its mission is to "lead, advocate for, and empower women of African descent, their families and communities." "Our organization promotes education; encourages entrepreneurship, financial and economic stability; educates women about health; promotes healthcare access and promotes civic engagement; also advocates for sound public policy and social justice."

In May of 2023, the Roselle chapter of the NCNW hosted a Mother's Day Luncheon and Fashion Show. It was the first time in four years that we hosted our Annual Mother's Day Luncheon due to the COVID-19 pandemic. Our president, the Rev. Naomi Myers, who is also Assistant Pastor of my church and local elder, organized a beautiful and successful event. While there were a few glitches, guests commented that it was a very nice event and they look forward to it next year.

Mother's Day is a day we honor all mothers and those who nurture, love, guide, and lead as mothers. History recognizes the efforts of Ann Jarvis as the woman who first wanted to honor mothers for the sacrifices they made for their children. Her first celebration was at a Methodist church. She persisted and in 1914, President Woodrow Wilson made the second Sunday in May an official Mother's Day holiday.

All of us have or had a mother. Some of us are mothers and some of us have adopted the role of mother for other family members or youth in need. God chose Mary to be with child – the one who was to be our Lord and Savior.

When the angel Gabriel visited Mary with the news that she would be the mother of Jesus, she only asked how this could be since she was a virgin. "With complete faith and acceptance." Mary added in Luke 1:38 (KJV), "Behold the handmaid of the Lord; be it unto me according to Thy word." Most Christians view Mary as blessed and highly favored because God chose her. She did not have an easy life. She endured difficult times like mothers today, but she is a great example of how God kept her through it all. Just like our AME pastors and teachers have always taught and encouraged us, God will take care of us through it all, no matter what the trial or tribulation, if we just trust Him.

In the 21st century, there are so many opportunities open to young women that many do not aspire to motherhood or aspire to it later in life. Sometimes, fathers are the ones who stay home and parent while their partner takes on the role of breadwinner. I am old school and think mothers have a paramount role of homemaker and raising children - the one who sets the example of Christian beliefs, demeanor, and conduct, probably because this was my experience. I'm sure there are Christian men who lead in setting the example of Christianity in their homes.

At the Mother's Day Luncheon, several women and one man were honored. The man was honored as Outstanding Community Leader, and he is without question someone young men should emulate. He is a husband and father who acknowledged the gift of his wife to him. Women were honored as Outstanding Educator, Business Woman Of the Year and NCNW Council Woman of the Year. Three young women who are currently students - two twin high school students and one college student - were honored as Outstanding Youth of the Year and Youth Leader of the Year, respectively. These three younger women have accomplishments in sports, education, religious activities, and community service. They are well on their way to a promising future. My prayer for them is that they always trust in God and pray at least once in their lives the following prayer I wrote at the beginning of 2023 from my favorite chair where I sometimes read, meditate, pray, and think:

> Jesus, be my Savior!
> Conquer my sins.
> Triumph over
> My enemies.
> Lift me up
> From any
> Pending despair.
>
> Clothe me
> In Your
> Righteousness.
> Feed me with
> Your peace and promises.

Touch me with
Your compassion and love.
Comfort me with
Your grace and mercy.
Guide me with
Your Word and works.
Speak to me
With Your spirit and wisdom.
Walk with me through the valley, up the mountains.

Ride with me on the highways and by-ways.
Sit with me
In my dining and meditations.
Lie with me
As I rest and slumber.
Be with me
As I rise and give thanks.
Jesus, be my Savior.

Taking Care of Oneself

Some homes are endowed with more sunlight than others. Owners appreciate and prefer this natural light. Its brightness adds to the spiritual peace and warmth of the rooms. It is favorable for reading, meditation, and daytime prayer. I can thank God for awakening me to a new day, a satisfying breakfast, and ultimately an entrance into the fresh air. Then, off to a vigorous workout at the YMCA - my enhanced fitness class that meets for an hour three days a week. We do aerobics, chair exercises, bending, and stretching. This, too, is part of my firm foundation as I seek to equip this body with what it needs to be healthy. Its members are connected to the larger body of the church whose purpose is to do the will of Jesus Christ.

Food is my greatest challenge. I like oatmeal

and fruit for breakfast, but I tire of it and end up getting avocado toast with bacon and sometimes, a blueberry muffin - not good. Once in a while, I prepare a spinach omelet with microwaved bacon. I very rarely eat fried foods, sometimes using my air fryer for chicken wings or turkey wings. I eat small portions of meat, fish and vegetables, mostly spinach and kale, and have a sweet potato. Rarely, I will have a baked white potato and chicken flavored rice with carrots and broccoli. I eat green salads and tuna, too. On really hot days, I sometimes opt for a sandwich with whole wheat bread and turkey, lettuce, and tomato or tuna, lettuce, and tomato, oil, and vinegar. I don't drink milk, juice, or coffee. I do like hot, unsweetened green tea or ginger tea. Snacks include popcorn, pistachio yogurt bars, ginger ale, dark chocolate, and naturally flavored jelly beans (I try to stick to those at Easter time). I drink plenty of water. My doctors tell me I am healthy and to keep doing whatever I am doing, but I know my body is not all it should be. Gastrointestinal problems persist. A holistic doctor warned me about dairy and sugary foods and drinks which means I should avoid the blueberry muffins, yogurt, and the candies. When we know better, we should do better. Help me, Jesus! Today is May 26th. I had a doctor's appointment today. The doctor told me to exercise, eat carefully, and to lose some weight. Don't I know it!

I think of my mother. I never once saw her very sick. I am sure she had health issues because the doctor would make house calls. That's when they were doing that sort of thing. She believed in moderation in all things. She set a good example. I wish I had adopted more of her ways. There are some things I disagreed with her about. Some were deeply rooted, but God saw me through it all. I am so thankful that Louise Hall Smith was my mother. My greatest joy, however, is knowing Jesus died for me and all of us and that He arose on the third day and I have the indwelling of the Holy Spirit and I am promised the gift of eternal life. Oh, to one day be with Him in glory!

"This little light of mine. Yes, I'm gonna to let it shine." The light of knowing Jesus as Lord and Savior and best friend. The light of worship and praise. The light of His God-given gifts to share. The light of service to others in need. Yes, I will let these shine until the day I go home to be with the Lord and my other transitioned family. This is the firm foundation that the Lord has made for me. Someone once told me the Bible said two is better than one. Well, in my house, Jesus and I are in the majority. Family and friends are just a prayer, a phone call, and a drive away.

Juneteenth and Father's Day

The eve of Juneteenth was Father's Day. My pastor preached a powerful sermon about being a real man. He assured the congregation that real men are not afraid to show emotion or to confess that they are sorry. They are strong, but not domineering. They profess their love, protect, and provide. They pray.

My father had quiet, inner strength. I never saw him angry or acting in a way that I would call ugly. I think he thought his place was to provide and that my mother should take care of the home - cleaning, cooking, and raising the children. I don't mean to imply that he ignored us, but he trusted her judgement and let her take the lead as far as my brothers and I were concerned. He did chastise us if she told him we needed a spanking. That scenario was really old-fashioned. He loved to take his family on drives. He loved gathering together with his siblings, in-laws, and children. He loved to read. He loved to talk politics with his friends. I never saw him pray, but I prayed with my mother as a young child.

Some of you may wonder why I am revisiting all of this in my mind. These are my roots, and if we don't acknowledge our roots, how can we truly know who we are today and look back and thank Jesus for how far we have come? My daily prayers now include more about the men in my family, my nephews, and cousins. I want them to be good husbands and fathers. I want them to be Christian in their beliefs, attitudes, and behavior, to know Jesus as Lord and Savior. I am not worried about the women in my family. Most of them have developed a relationship with Christ and belong to a church where they can have worship, praise, and engage in service and fellowship.

On the eve of Juneteenth, I am thinking

about President Biden making it a federal holiday in 2021. It was a long time coming, but it happened. We have documentation that we as a people are free, but the reality is we have come far, but still have so much farther to go. Will we ever be free as long as there is hate in the hearts of men and women who want to destroy Black people and keep us down? I think about the death of those nine people in a South Carolina church who were gunned down while having prayer; the death of those ten people in a shopping center in a mostly Black neighborhood in Buffalo, New York gunned down; the near fatal shooting of a young Black teenager who mistakenly went to the wrong house to pick up his sibling and rang the doorbell. That's just to mention only three of so many senseless, hateful crimes in this nation against Black people.

Should Black people be appeased by or feel grateful for the appointments of a Black woman Vice President or a Black woman on the

Supreme Court? A Black man having served as a U.S. President and a Black First Lady? Surely these individuals have felt gratitude and victory, but were not appeased. The Black community in America as a whole should continue to work and pray and lift each other up.

Asians and Jews have also died and suffered from the attacks of haters in recent years. The LGBTQ community has also been victimized. Banning books won't stop people from being who they truly are. It won't keep them from telling their stories.

Fantasy vs. Reality

I have fantasized about being named poet laureate, or walking into a bookstore and seeing my name on the bookshelf. While I have given up on the first, the latter is still in my heart. I celebrate the accomplishments of poet and author Amanda Gorman. I pray for her and those young people in high schools and colleges across the country who have a gift of writing and a desire to share it with others. I have found joy and contentment in sharing more with others those things in my life that might prove helpful and encouraging to youth and adults. I love the written word and the spoken word. I find myself drawn to people who have gifts for both. I seem to have an affinity for them. That's why I love the Bible and participate in Bible study - The Word of

God, so all-encompassing and powerful, a road map for living.

Still, another thing I have fantasized about is a new home. This townhouse I now occupy has been my home for 15 years - the neighborhood has been my home for 29 years. There have been times I have felt very uncomfortable and even unsafe here, and other times, very secure and happy. In Bible study, I have learned, especially from those that are my senior, that the more you try to live a Christian life, the more Satan, the enemy, tries to attack. It's not easy being a Christian and living alone with your energies and loyalties spread out in several directions, especially in your senior citizen years.

On the one hand, I am thinking better is the enemy you know than the one you don't know, and the Holy Spirit is telling me to be grateful and content with what I have and to be a good steward over it. I am trusting the Holy Spirit until it tells me something different and at the same time, I am intent on being ready if it tells me to make a change. Until then, Jesus and I are the majority here in my home.

Helping Our Youth

Fellow seniors, we've got to read the signs of the young people in our lives, hear the sighs and inner cries for attention and help. Then we can discern what is truly needed and how best to supply it. Can we take off the masks and show our real selves, the truth and vulnerability that lies behind them? Yes, it may be necessary to do just that in order to win a victory for Christ.

Here are some key questions for youth who may want to know if they are positioning themselves in obedience to God:

1. Am I really comfortable wearing this outfit?
2. Are the song lyrics to this music worthy of my attention?
3. How much influence on me do my peers have?

4. Is this a place where I should be going?
5. Is omitting a truth the same as lying?
6. Are the words I speak positive, uplifting, and encouraging?
7. Is it ever ok to take something that belongs to someone else?
8. Does this have the potential to harm my body?

Remember also, God want us to experience joy. We don't need to be so rigid in our thinking that we can't relax, have fun, and enjoy peace of mind. I didn't graduate from a school of divinity or attain any theological education. I don't claim to have any authority in teaching the Bible, but being a child of God has afforded me the opportunity to know some things.

Since my husband's death, the women in my life have played a major role. Their words, actions, and lifestyles have set an example for me. Like Michelle Obama wrote in her book

The Light We Carry, "Each of us carries a bit of brightness, something entirely unique and individual, a flame worth protecting." These women have let their light shine through decades of service to others. We've all been married and have buried husbands. We've experienced the challenges that marriage brings and the energies it takes to make it work.

I say to the young ladies and young men who are thinking about the future in regard to marriage and parenthood, "Stand up for something or fall for anything." Don't be anxious about the future. Tomorrow will take care of itself. Ask Jesus to help you find someone with whom to share your life. Remember the scripture, "Seek first the Kingdom and His righteousness and all things will be added unto you." Matthew 6:33 (NIV) To the young men, I lift up the scripture, "He who finds a wife, finds that which is good and receives favor from the Lord." Proverbs 18:22 (NIV)

Since the deaths of my immediate family members and that of my husband, I have had to participate in grief counseling. I want to say there is nothing to be ashamed of if you need mental or emotional health services. Rather, be glad there are professionals who can be objective and know the intricate workings of the mind and body. Yes, Jesus knows this, but sometimes He sends a messenger to aid you. I had the help of two professionals before finding a third who was best for me. I am so grateful and assured that I can make it through my journey to a graceful ending. Also, I am certain in my heart that the young people in my church will one day say to themselves and maybe to others: I am glad I believed. I am glad I had faith.

"We must accept those things we cannot change and change those things we can…" In the beginning, the coronavirus was out of our control until the experts researched, studied, and discovered vaccines. Now, these fires starting in

Canada are threatening the air we breathe. We see in these instances our lack of control over things that threaten our health and safety. Despite what scientists and meteorologists say, we cannot by far rule out prayer as an answer to how to respond and cope. To youth, I say in closing, by the time you're half my age, it may be another type of pandemic. Whatever the future holds, know who holds the future and remember these words - "Joy cometh in the morning."

What is your firm foundation? Is it a building or a heart, mind and soul for Christ? Are you living according to His will or have you been self-seeking? The Christian life is not an easy life, but a good one. We laugh, We cry. We pray. We endure. We fail. We succeed. We fall down. We get back up. We stand. As the song lyrics say, "We build our hopes on things eternal. So, "Hold onto God's unchanging hands."

Book Summary

This book is about Christian living and the establishing of a firm foundation in one's home and life based on belief in Jesus Christ and His Word, the Bible. It addresses young people who may be aspiring to higher education, young adults, parents who are raising children, and seniors. It focuses on what truly matters, finding the source of grace and mercy during challenging times and taking care of oneself. The author believes that with such a foundation you will not only survive, but triumph and experience victory.

About the Author

The author has self-published 13 books, including this one, all poetry except for one. The book, *Testimony: the T's Have It*, tells her story. This book, *Just As A House On A Firm Foundation*, is best described as part two of her testimony as she takes on a familiar subject and makes it her own.

In addition to her writing books, the author is also editor of the Heard Herald Quarterly, her church's newsletter. This task - one she thoroughly enjoys - is a public relations outreach of the church Historical Commission, a ministry that she serves.

Although she has achieved in the area of education, she places it secondary to being a child of God with a calling. She is especially proud of the Christian poetry that she has publicly shared in a few of her other books. To God be the glory!